What We Have in Common

A Brim Coloring Book
Written by Jane Landey
Edited by David Austin
Drawings by David Austin and Jane Austin

Copyright©2017

Published by CreateSpace: An Amazon Company.
Printed in U.S.A.

Introduction

What We Have in Common. Brim Coloring books enable children to color the drawings as they read along! They display the similarities of related animals. In this series, the buffalo and the bull are compared. The facts enable children to appreciate common values. Thus, imbibing in them interest towards animals which could help them appreciate what they have in common with one another.

The Buffalo

And

The Bull

The buffalo and the bull meet on a farm.

I am a buffalo.

I am a bull.

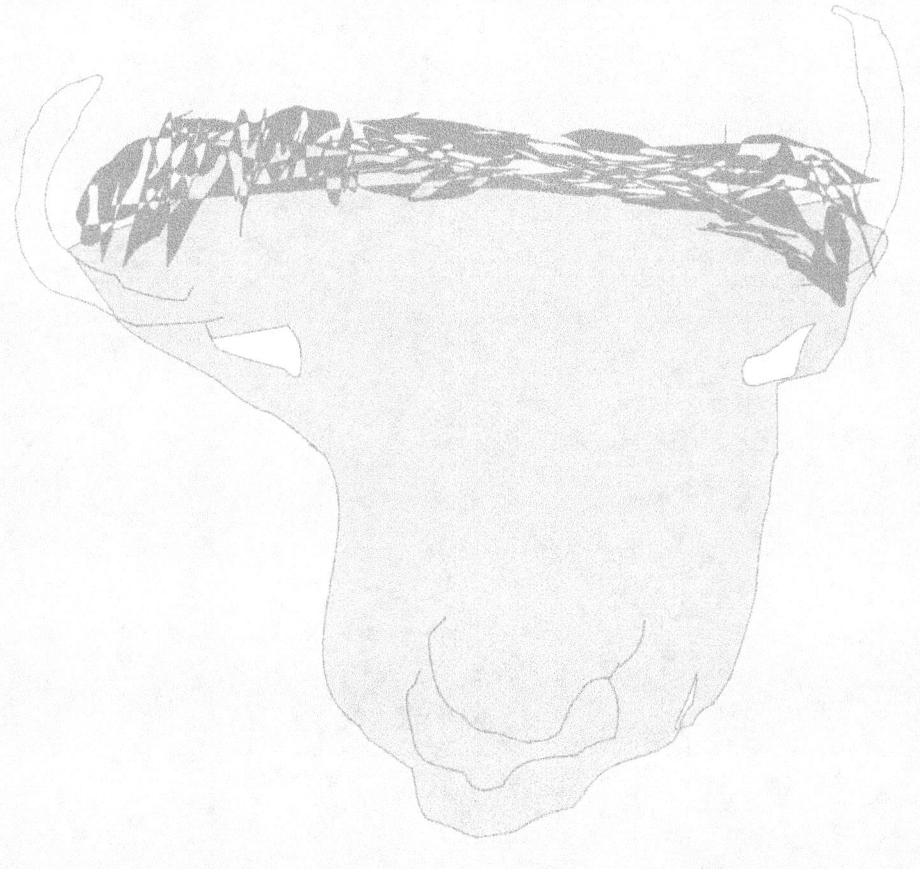

I have horns.

I have thick horns too!

I have thick skin.

I have thick skin too!

I fight with my horns.

I fight with mine too!

Let's fight!

My horns can't hit hard enough.

Mine too!

Hold it.

Alright enough!

I win.

Can you run like me?

Ready? We go!

Run! Run! Run!

Oh, you are faster!

Alright, I will run slowly!

I cannot run as fast as you do!

What game do you like?

Horn game. I mean fighting with my
horns.

My horns are shorter than yours!

I can push you with my horns.

I can move back!

Do you want to play the horn game?

Yes I am ready!

Here I come!

Have a kick too!

Alright have a blow!

I can move back!

I can kick with my horns!

And I can kick with my hind legs too!

What We Have in Common Brim Coloring Books

Crocodile and Alligator
Turtle and Tortoise
Starfish and Octopus
Worm and Snake
Turkey and Vulture
Ostrich and Emu
Weka and Kiwi
Bat and Rat
Camel and Llama
Duck and Pelican
Kangaroo and Wallaby
Pig and Tapir
Skunk and Squirrel
Hedge and Anteater
Cat and Owl
Elephant and Rhinoceros
Dog and Fox
Buffalo and Bull
Leopard and Cheetah
Horse and Zebra